Football

in Action

John Crossingham

 Crabtree Publishing Company
www.crabtreebooks.com

Created by Bobbie Kalman

**For my good friend Todd,
who is probably surprised to be reading this**

Editor-in-Chief
Bobbie Kalman

Author
John Crossingham

Managing editor
Lynda Hale

Editors
Kate Calder
Hannelore Sotzek
Niki Walker

Copy editors
Heather Fitzpatrik
Amanda Bishop

Computer design
John Crossingham
Lynda Hale

Consultant
Sam Mutz, Eastern Director,
Pop Warner Little Scholars

Special thanks to
John Jasenovsky; Jon Butler, Ron Dilatush, and Pop Warner Little Scholars

Photographs
Courtesy of Pop Warner Little Scholars: pages 4-5, 13, 14, 15, 28
SportsChrome: Brian Drake: title page, pages 25, 27; Rob Tringali Jr.: pages 12, 20
Other images by Digital Stock and Eyewire, Inc.

Illustrations
All illustration by Bonna Rouse except the following: David Calder:
pages 2 (border), 6, 7 (top and middle), 10-11, 13, 15; John Crossingham:
page 21 (bottom); Trevor Morgan: page 7 (bottom)

Production coordinator
Hannelore Sotzek

Digtial prepress
Embassy Graphics

Printer
Worzalla Publishing Company

Every reasonable effort has been made in obtaining authorization, where necessary, to publish images of the athletes who appear in this book. The publishers would be pleased to have any oversights or omissions brought
to their attention so that they may be corrected for subsequent printings.

Crabtree Publishing Company

www.crabtreebooks.com   1-800-387-7650

Cataloging in Publication Data
Crossingham, John, 1974-
    Football in action

p. cm. —(Sports in action)
Includes index.

ISBN 0-7787-0166-2 (library bound) ISBN 0-7787-0178-6 (pbk.)
This book introduces the techniques, rules, equipment, and safety requirements of football.

1. Football—Juvenile literature. [1. Football.] I. Title. II. Series: Kalman, Bobbie. Sports in action.

GV950.7 .c76 2001   j796.332—dc21   LC 00-057076
                                                                           CIP

**Published in
the United States**
PMB 16A
350 Fifth Ave.
Suite 3308
New York, NY
10118

**Published
in Canada**
616 Welland Ave.,
St. Catharines,
Ontario, Canada
L2M 5V6

**Published in the
United Kingdom**
73 Lime Walk
Headington
Oxford
0X3 7AD
United Kingdom

**Published
in Australia**
386 Mt. Alexander Rd.,
Ascot Vale (Melbourne)
V1C 3032

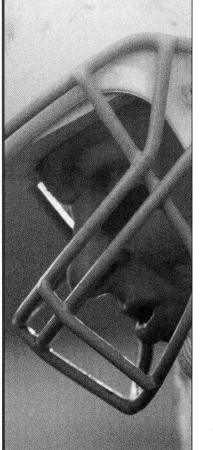

Contents

What is Football?

Football is one of North America's most popular team sports. The object of the game is to score points by carrying or kicking the ball into the opposing team's **end zone**. The team that scores the most points wins. Football players run, pass, and push as they try to score and stop their opponents from scoring.

Four quarters make a match

Professional football games are divided into four fifteen-minute sections called **quarters**. In high school, quarters are twelve minutes long. If the score is tied after four quarters, teams play extra five-minute periods called **overtime** until one team scores. In youth leagues, quarters last only eight minutes. Instead of overtime, teams play a **Kansas City Tie-Breaker** in which each team gets four chances to score and break the tie.

The birth of football

In the late 1800s, the game of **rugby** was a popular sport. Rugby players scored points by carrying the ball over lines at the end of the field. In 1880, an American named Walter Camp made changes to rugby to make the game more organized. For example, teams now had to line up facing one another and wait for a count before they could move. Camp's version of rugby became football.

Offense and defense

A team can have many players, but only eleven may play on the field at once. The team that has control of the ball is playing **offense**. Its players try to score by running and passing the ball toward the end zone.

The team without control of the ball is playing **defense**. Its members try to gain control of the ball and stop their opponents from scoring points. Both teams have offensive and defensive players.

The Essentials

Football players are pushed and **tackled**, or grabbed and brought down to the ground. They need a lot of protective equipment. This gear can be expensive, but you will not hear the players complain about it! Football is a rough sport, so protection is taken seriously—even during a practice. If you are not wearing all the proper equipment, the referee will not let you play.

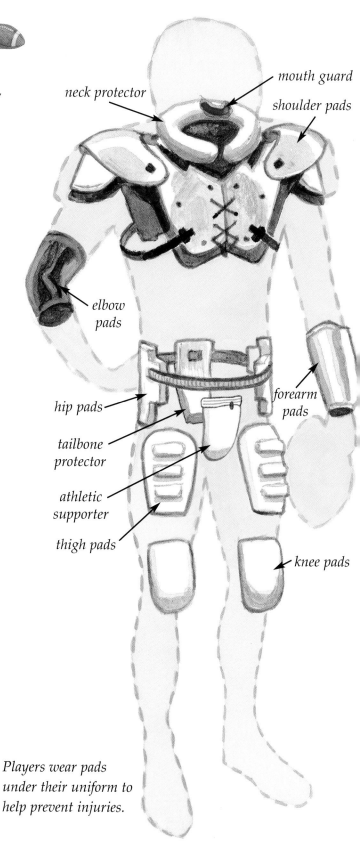

neck protector

mouth guard

shoulder pads

elbow pads

hip pads

tailbone protector

athletic supporter

thigh pads

forearm pads

knee pads

Players wear pads under their uniform to help prevent injuries.

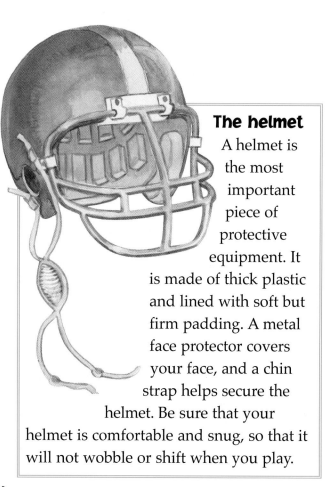

The helmet

A helmet is the most important piece of protective equipment. It is made of thick plastic and lined with soft but firm padding. A metal face protector covers your face, and a chin strap helps secure the helmet. Be sure that your helmet is comfortable and snug, so that it will not wobble or shift when you play.

6

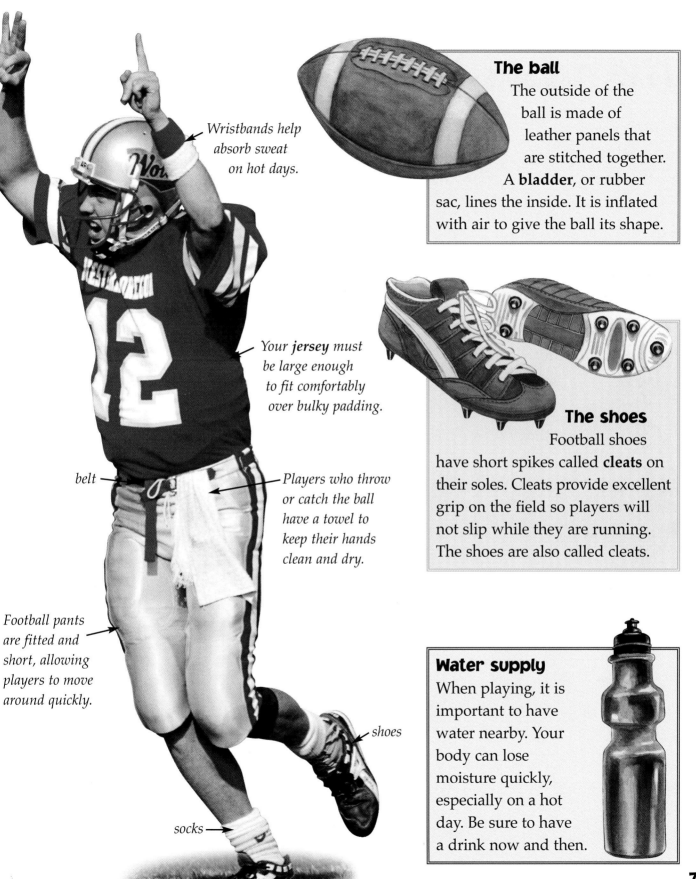

Wristbands help absorb sweat on hot days.

The ball
The outside of the ball is made of leather panels that are stitched together. A **bladder**, or rubber sac, lines the inside. It is inflated with air to give the ball its shape.

Your **jersey** must be large enough to fit comfortably over bulky padding.

belt

Players who throw or catch the ball have a towel to keep their hands clean and dry.

The shoes
Football shoes have short spikes called **cleats** on their soles. Cleats provide excellent grip on the field so players will not slip while they are running. The shoes are also called cleats.

Football pants are fitted and short, allowing players to move around quickly.

shoes

Water supply
When playing, it is important to have water nearby. Your body can lose moisture quickly, especially on a hot day. Be sure to have a drink now and then.

socks

7

Warming Up

Before practicing or playing, it is important to stretch and warm up your muscles. Warming up loosens your muscles so you move better, and it helps prevent injuries such as muscle strains and pulls. Move slowly, never bounce, and never stretch more than feels comfortable.

Trunk Circles
Place your feet shoulder-width apart, and put your hands on your hips. Keep your feet flat on the ground and swing your hips around in circles. Do three circles to the right and three to the left.

Arm Circles
Swing your arms in large circles. Make the circles smaller and smaller until your arms are moving in tiny circles straight out to the side. Reverse the direction, starting with small circles and ending with giant ones.

Neck Stretch
It is easy to hurt your neck, so do this stretch carefully. Tilt your head forward so that your chin points at your chest. Now slowly move your head toward one shoulder and then the other. Do not roll your head backward or farther than feels comfortable.

Quadriceps Stretch

Stand on your left foot and use your left hand to support yourself against a wall. Bring your right foot up behind you until you can grab it with your right hand. Pull gently until you feel the stretch in the front of your leg. Hold the stretch for a count of ten and then stretch your left leg.

Ankle Stretch

Sit on the ground with one leg straight. Bend your other leg so that you can grab your foot. Gently move it in circles. When you have done ten, stop and do ten circles in the other direction. Change legs!

Leg Lunges

Stand with your feet wide apart. Bend your left knee until you feel a stretch on the inside of your right leg. Hold the stretch for a count of five. Straighten up and switch sides.

"V" Stretch

Sit with your legs in a "V." Stretch your arms out in front of you until you feel a stretch in the back of your legs and buttocks. Hold the stretch for a count of ten.

Welcome to the Field

Football is played on a rectangular field. The field is 120 yards (110 m) long and 160 feet (49 m) wide. There are two end zones found on the last ten yards (9 m) of each end of the field. Teams defend their end zone against opponents trying to score a **touchdown**, which is worth six points. A touchdown is scored when a player catches or carries the ball into the opposing team's end zone.

After scoring a touchdown, a team has the chance to score a **conversion**. There are two types of conversions. The first is the **one-point conversion**, or **point after**, in which the kicker kicks the ball between the **goal posts**. The second is the **two-point conversion**, in which the team starts at the three-yard line and has one chance to run or pass the ball past its opponents and into the end zone.

The kickoff

Games begin with a **kickoff**, shown right. Before the game, the teams flip a coin. The team that wins the coin toss chooses whether it will kick or receive. A player from the kicking team, called the **kicker**, makes the kickoff. He or she kicks the ball, which is mounted on a rubber **tee**, as shown above. Players on the receiving team, called **return players**, catch the ball.

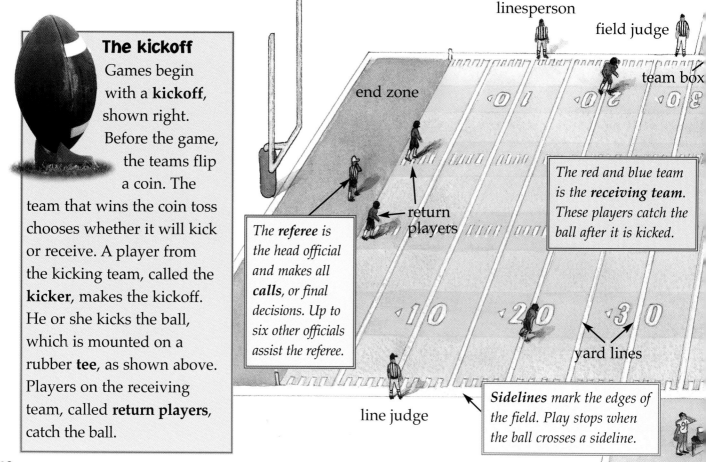

linesperson

field judge

end zone

team box

The referee is the head official and makes all calls, or final decisions. Up to six other officials assist the referee.

return players

The red and blue team is the receiving team. These players catch the ball after it is kicked.

yard lines

line judge

Sidelines mark the edges of the field. Play stops when the ball crosses a sideline.

10

Get down

The offense has four **downs**, or chances, to move the ball at least ten yards. The defense tries to stop them by tackling the player who is carrying the ball. If the team moves the ball ten yards, it is given a new **first down**. Now the offense has four new downs in which to move the ball another ten yards. If a team runs out of downs before moving the ball ten yards, its opponents gain possession of the ball.

Use your boot

Rather than risk losing the ball at its present position, a team on a fourth down can choose to kick the ball. If the team is close enough to the goal posts, it may kick a **field goal**, which is worth three points. To score a field goal, the kicker kicks the ball between the other team's goal posts. The team may also **punt**, or kick the ball toward the other team's end zone. For more on field goals and punting, see page 26.

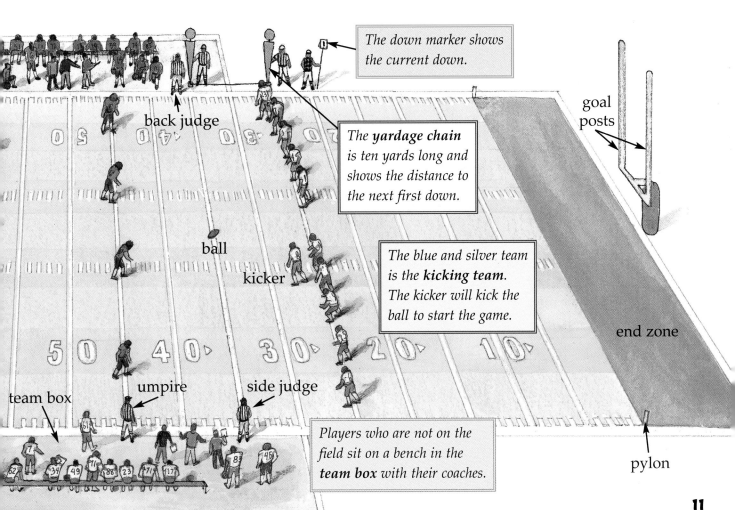

back judge

The down marker shows the current down.

The **yardage chain** is ten yards long and shows the distance to the next first down.

ball

kicker

The blue and silver team is the **kicking team**. The kicker will kick the ball to start the game.

goal posts

end zone

team box

umpire

side judge

Players who are not on the field sit on a bench in the **team box** with their coaches.

pylon

11

Offense—Moving Forward

A team's offensive players have one major objective—keep moving forward! When they advance, they not only make first downs and keep possession of the ball, they also get closer to the end zone and to scoring a touchdown. The act of advancing forward is called a **drive**. Each of the eleven offensive positions has a specific duty to help execute a drive.

At the beginning of each down, the referee places the ball at the **line of scrimmage**. This imaginary line crosses the field where the ball was stopped by the defense on the last down. The teams line up facing each other at this line. No player may cross the line until the **center** of the offensive team **snaps** the ball, or tosses it back, to the **quarterback**.

Offensive layout

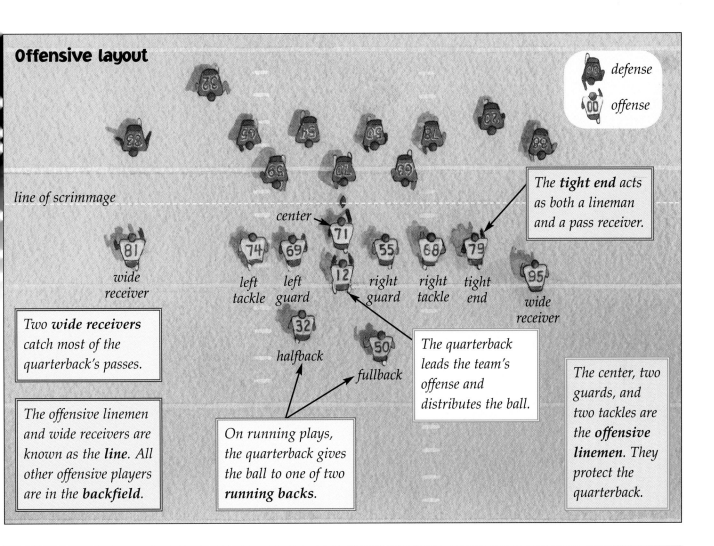

line of scrimmage

center

The **tight end** acts as both a lineman and a pass receiver.

81
wide receiver

74
left tackle

69
left guard

71

12

55
right guard

68
right tackle

79
tight end

95
wide receiver

32
halfback

50
fullback

defense

offense

Two **wide receivers** catch most of the quarterback's passes.

The quarterback leads the team's offense and distributes the ball.

The offensive linemen and wide receivers are known as the **line**. All other offensive players are in the **backfield**.

On running plays, the quarterback gives the ball to one of two **running backs**.

The center, two guards, and two tackles are the **offensive linemen**. They protect the quarterback.

Special teams

Special teams are formations of players used when a team punts or attempts a field goal. Most players on special teams also have an offensive or defensive position. These teams include **field goal units**, **punting units**, and **return units**. Here are some positions:

kicker: This player kicks the ball at kickoff, punts, and field goals.

holder: The holder steadies the ball for the kicker during attempts at field goals.

return player: This person catches punts from the opposition and runs with them toward the end zone.

Defense—None Shall Pass!

Defensive players try to stop their opponents from moving forward and scoring. Each defensive player has an opponent to **cover**, or guard closely, to stop them from passing or running. The defense must be ready for any type of play the other team uses. Sometimes defensive players **blitz**, or rush forward in a large group, to surprise the opposing quarterback while he or she still has the ball. The blitz will often stop their opponent's attack before it even starts! The defense has a **captain** who leads and organizes his or her teammates. This player is usually one of the team's linebackers.

Defensive layout

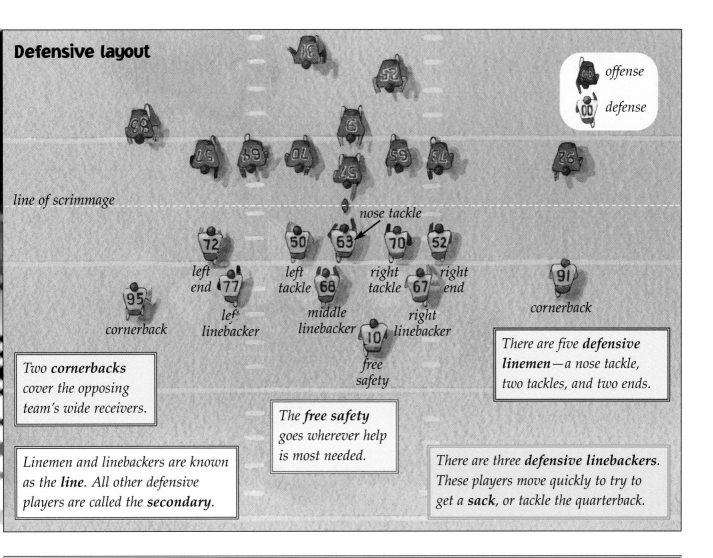

offense

defense

line of scrimmage

nose tackle

72 left end

77 left linebacker

50 left tackle

68

63

70 right tackle

67

52 right end

10 free safety

right linebacker

middle linebacker

91 cornerback

95 cornerback

Two **cornerbacks** cover the opposing team's wide receivers.

Linemen and linebackers are known as the **line**. All other defensive players are called the **secondary**.

The **free safety** goes wherever help is most needed.

There are five **defensive linemen**—a nose tackle, two tackles, and two ends.

There are three **defensive linebackers**. These players move quickly to try to get a **sack**, or tackle the quarterback.

The defense can score, too

Defensive players are able to score in two ways:

1. If a defender **intercepts**, or catches an opponent's pass, he or she can score a touchdown by running into the opponent's end zone.

2. A **safety** is not just a position—it is also a play that scores two points. When an opponent has the ball in his or her own end zone and is tackled by a defender, the defense scores a safety. This happens only when a team must begin its drive deep in its own end.

Quarterbacks must often retreat to avoid the defense. This action sometimes leads to a safety.

Huddle, Count, Snap!

The offense must be well organized to get past the defensive players. Offensive players learn a variety of attack plans called **plays**. Plays are offensive strategies used to get the ball past the defense and into the end zone. The defense also uses plays to stop the offense. Before every down, the offense has a quick meeting called a **huddle**. The quarterback tells the players which play they are going to use. Players must remember their job in every play. The quarterback also tells the team what the **count** will be.

The count is a secret series of numbers and words that the quarterback shouts at the start of every down. "32, 17, 57, hut!" is an example of a count. The numbers are a code that acts as a reminder of the play. When the quarterback comes to the end of the count, the center snaps the ball and the play begins. Only the offense knows when the count will end. The players are ready to move the instant the center snaps the ball. The defense watches the ball and is usually a split-second behind the offensive players.

Snap to it

The snap should be fast and accurate. A good snap allows the center to concentrate on blocking the defense and gives the quarterback time to make a smooth play. You can practice the snap with a friend.

quarterback

center

1. The quarterback waits for the snap with hands relaxed and open, ready to receive the football.

The center grips the front half of the ball by forming a "V" with his or her thumb and fingers, while watching the opposing nose tackle.

2. Once the ball is snapped, the quarterback gets a good grip before pulling it back toward his or her chest and preparing to throw or pass the ball.

nose tackle

After the center releases the ball, he or she rushes forward to block the nose tackle.

Running with the Ball

Running plays are the most common methods of attack, especially in youth football. The quarterback hands the ball to a running back, who then runs as far as possible toward the end zone before getting tackled. A smart runner always looks for gaps to slip through in the defensive line.

When you get tackled, the play does not end until one of your knees touches the ground. At this point, you are **down**. The referee blows the whistle to say that the play is **dead**, or stopped. If you drop the football before the play is dead, it is a **fumble**. The first team to grab the loose ball gains possession of it.

Receiving the handoff

When taking the ball, grab it with both hands and bring it toward your body. Place the hand that is nearest to the quarterback over the ball and the other hand underneath.

Giving the handoff

Hold the ball near one end so your hands will not get in the running back's way. Extend your arms and place the ball into the running back's hands at chest level.

Opposing linemen attempt to sack the quarterback. A quick, smooth handoff allows the quarterback to move the ball before he or she is tackled.

Carrying the ball

After you grab the ball, you will become the main target of the defensive players. They will not only try to tackle you—they will try to **strip**, or grab, the ball from your hands. To shield the ball, hold one end of it with one hand and press the other end firmly into your armpit.

Have your free hand outstretched to help keep your balance while running.

Protecting the ball

While running, hold the football snugly against your chest. When moving through a group of defenders, bring the ball to the middle of your chest and cross both arms over it.

Breaking tackles

Even the trickiest, fastest running backs get caught by the defense. Since you are bound to get tackled, it is important to know how to gain extra yards even after you have been grabbed. Here are a few things you can do to keep moving forward.

Hold your free arm straight out toward the tackler. Use it to fend off your opponent. This position is called a **straightarm**, and only players carrying the ball are allowed to use it.

A sudden change of direction can puzzle your tackler. If you see a defender coming, move toward that player. Just as the defender lunges at you, turn slightly and run around him or her.

If there is no way to avoid a tackle, go straight into it and keep on running. Imagine trying to go through your opponent!

Hold the ball in your throwing hand. Your forefinger sits between the laces and the tip of the ball, and the other three fingers touch the laces. Your thumb rests across from your forefinger on the other side of the ball.

Passing

Passing plays are the quickest way to move the ball a long distance. They are trickier than running plays, however. Successful passing requires good communication between the quarterback and the receiver. If the receiver is not ready, the pass may be intercepted or **incomplete**, or missed. Receivers must get into position quickly—the quarterback can get sacked while waiting for a receiver to be ready to catch the ball.

Throwing the ball

*As you throw, flick your wrist down to put a **spin** on the ball. The spin makes the ball easier to catch.*

1. Grip the ball in your right hand (see page 20). Use your left hand to steady the ball. When you are ready to pass, bring your right arm back. Move your left arm in front of you for balance. Step forward and shift your weight to your left foot.

2. Bring the ball behind your head. Quickly bring your right arm over your head in an **arc**, or curve. Release the ball at the top of the arc. Your body weight is now fully on your left foot. Your right heel is raised.

These are right-handed instructions. For lefties, simply use the reverse.

Rules of passing

Here are some important rules for passing:

Only players in the backfield or at the ends of the line can receive a pass—they are the **eligible receivers**. In the example below, the right wide receiver has moved back from the line. Now, the tight end is at one end of the line and becomes an eligible receiver as well.

line of scrimmage

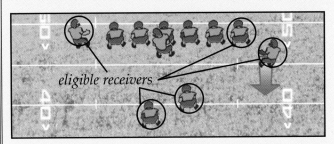

eligible receivers

Once the quarterback (blue circle) crosses the line of scrimmage, he or she cannot make any forward passes. The quarterback can make a **lateral** to the running back (yellow circle). A lateral is a pass that is thrown backward—never forward.

Receiving

There is much more to receiving than just catching the ball—you must first be **open**, or available to make the catch. As a receiver, you will have cornerbacks and free safeties hounding you even before you receive the ball. Fortunately, there are a number of moves you can use to avoid the defense and get open long enough to receive the pass.

Getting open

1. Charge toward the defender but do not run at full speed. This move should get the defender to move backward so that he or she is a little off-balance.

2. While the defender is moving backward, quickly change direction. This move is called **breaking for the pass**. Turn left or right to face the quarterback. Since your defender is off-balance, he or she will find it difficult to stay with you as you break.

3. You can also try to **fake** the defender. If you wish to break to your right, fake by moving a few steps to your left. As the defender starts to follow you, break to your right at full speed. Once you break, focus on receiving the pass from the quarterback.

Catching the pass

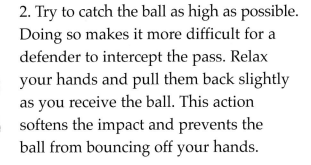

1. As you run to meet the ball, wait patiently before lifting your hands. When the ball is close, lift your hands to shoulder level and keep your palms open and up. Your thumbs should be pointing inward. Focus on the ball.

2. Try to catch the ball as high as possible. Doing so makes it more difficult for a defender to intercept the pass. Relax your hands and pull them back slightly as you receive the ball. This action softens the impact and prevents the ball from bouncing off your hands.

Alert eyes, soft hands

A good catch begins with the eyes, not the hands. Once the ball leaves the quarterback's fingers, do not take your eyes off it. Be relaxed—stiff hands and rigid movements will make the ball bounce out of your grasp.

3. As soon as you catch the ball, bring it firmly to your chest (see page 19). You may be tackled right after receiving the pass, and you do not want to fumble the ball! If you do not get tackled, run as fast as you can toward the end zone!

Blocking

Offensive linemen block their opponents to give their quarterback time to pass. They also clear a path for the running back as he or she heads for the end zone.

Empty pocket

On a passing play, the offensive linemen block defenders to create a **pocket** around the quarterback. The pocket is an area that is free of defenders. The longer the linemen can keep the pocket "empty," the more time the quarterback has to line up an accurate pass.

*(above) Linemen start each play from the **three-point stance**. Place one hand on the ground and keep your head up. Lean your body forward at the waist but keep your back straight.*

Open the hole

On running plays, the linemen try to make a hole in the opponent's defensive line. Several linemen work together to block a group of defenders. The running back then slips through the space without getting tackled. Sometimes both guards do a **sweep** block. They both block one side of the defense so the running back can run around it.

A blocking drill

Draw two lines, ten large steps apart. Have a friend act as a defender and stand with him or her between the lines. The defender tries to cross the line behind you, and you try to move your friend back across the line behind him or her.

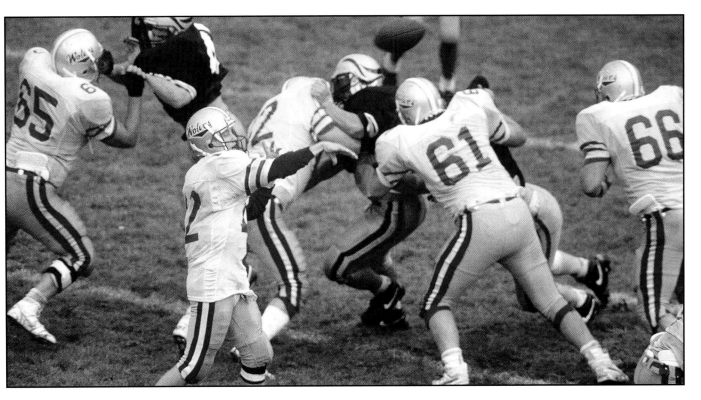

These linemen have created a comfortable pocket from which their quarterback can pass.

Making a block

1. Wait in the three-point stance. As soon as the quarterback finishes the count, move forward to meet your opponent. Keep your body slightly crouched and your palms open and facing forward.

2. As you make contact, keep both feet on the ground. Extend your body and give a quick shove to your opponent's chest with your arms. This move will knock the player backward and off balance.

3. Use quick, upward shoves to drive your opponent backward. Keep your body between the defender and the ball.

Kick It!

On fourth down, a team has three choices—punt, try a field goal, or continue the drive for a first down or touchdown. Continuing the drive is risky. If the team fails to get a new first down, the other team gets the ball at the line of scrimmage. Usually, the team chooses to punt instead. By punting, it can send the ball far down the field. This action puts the ball close to the opposition's end zone. The team's opponents now have farther to go for a touchdown.

Time to punt

In a punt, the center snaps the ball to the punter rather than the quarterback. When you are punting, wait for the ball ten yards behind the center. Stand relaxed with your hands ready to catch the ball.

1. Catch the ball and quickly turn it so that the laces face up. Extend your arms so the ball is in front of your waist. Take a step forward with your kicking foot. As you start a long step with your other foot, open your hands and drop the ball out in front of your kicking leg.

2. Swing your kicking leg forward so your foot meets the ball about a foot off the ground. Kick the center of the ball using your **instep**. Your instep is the top surface of your foot near your big toe.

Keep your eye on the ball throughout the entire punt. Do not worry about the action around you.

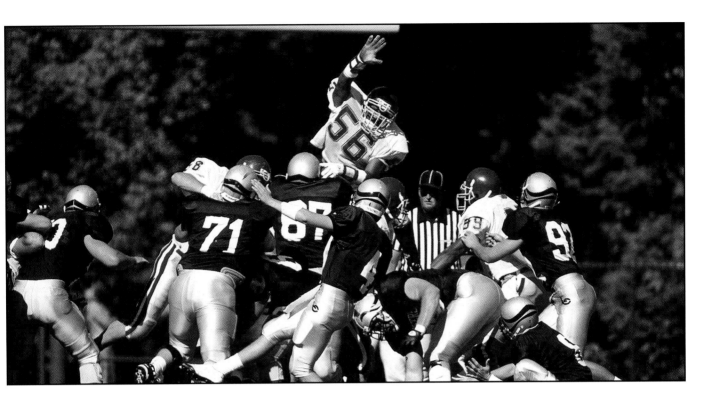

Kicking a field goal

If a team on a fourth down is within 35 yards of the goal posts, it may choose to attempt a field goal. On a field-goal attempt, the center snaps the ball to the **holder**. The holder kneels about five yards behind the center. He or she catches the snap and quickly sets up the ball for the kicker to kick.

1. Stand two or three large steps behind the holder. (Right-footed kickers stand slightly to the left of the holder—left-footed kickers stand to the right.)

2. Step quickly toward the ball and finish with your **plant foot**, shown right, next to the ball. The toe of your plant foot should point at the goal posts.

3. Kick the ball in the middle of the bottom stripe. **Follow through**, or continue swinging your leg, to ensure a powerful kick that will send the ball high.

(above) The field-goal attempt must be smooth and quick. Defenders will jump up and try to block your kick.

kicker

holder

plant foot

The holder uses one finger to steady the ball for the kicker. The ball's laces face forward.

Tackling

Tackling is a major part of football. All defensive players must be good tacklers in order to stop their opponents from scoring. Tackling is not easy. It is difficult to bring your opponent to the ground. Before you can tackle the ball carrier, you will have to fight your way through offensive blocks. This technique is called **shedding the blocker**.

When tackling your opponent, remember to grab and slap the ball until the whistle sounds. If you can make the player fumble, your team can get possession.

Shedding the blocker

The offensive linemen will try to block you and knock you back to protect the ball carrier. When approaching a lineman, crouch slightly and run directly at the player. As you reach the lineman, shift quickly toward one side. Get your arms underneath your opponent's arm. Shove your opponent to the side by throwing your arms and upper body upward. Now move toward the ball carrier to make a tackle.

Bring 'em down

The important thing about tackling is to get both of the ball carrier's feet off the ground so he or she is certain to fall. When some players tackle, they grab their opponent around the upper body and push. In this position, however, the ball carrier's feet are still on the ground. The opponent can twist and break free. Remember, play does not stop until the ball carrier's knee touches the ground.

As you grab the ball carrier, try to jolt his or her body up quickly. This motion lifts the player's feet off the ground. Immediately afterward, pull the player to the ground.

Tackle notes

The opponent's belt area is the best place to aim your tackle. Runners can fake you by moving their eyes, head, arms, and legs. The belt area, or **midsection**, is a stationary target on a runner.

A **flying tackle** may stop your opponent, but there is a good chance you will miss your target if the player moves after you jump.

NEVER hit another player with your head. Even though you are wearing a helmet, you can be badly injured! Make contact with your opponent using your shoulder instead.

In a game, tackles will not be smooth or easy. Remember! Football is a team sport. Do whatever you can to slow down the ball carrier. Soon your teammates will be there to help out.

ALWAYS keep your head up and eyes focused on the ball carrier when making a tackle.

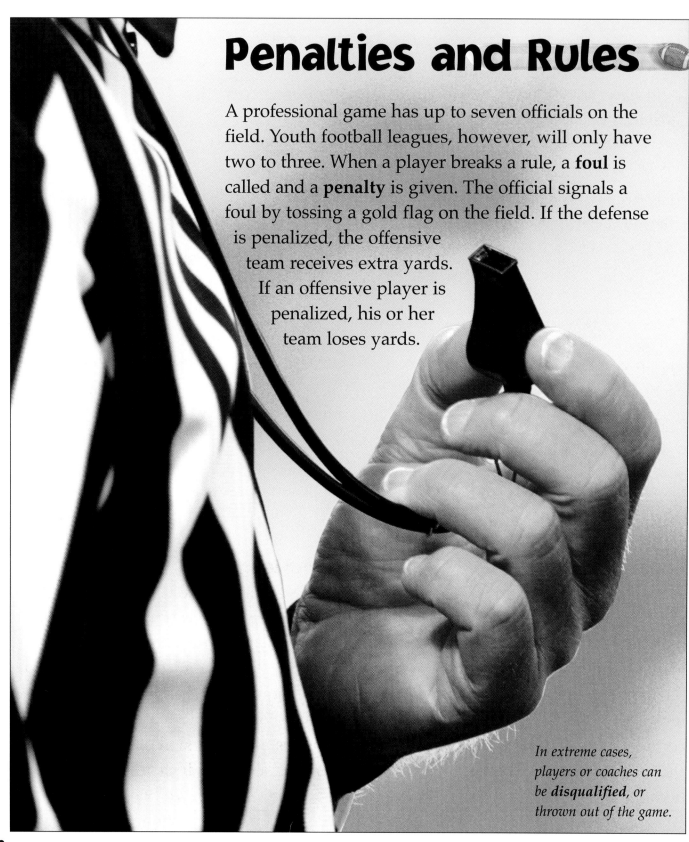

Penalties and Rules

A professional game has up to seven officials on the field. Youth football leagues, however, will only have two to three. When a player breaks a rule, a **foul** is called and a **penalty** is given. The official signals a foul by tossing a gold flag on the field. If the defense is penalized, the offensive team receives extra yards. If an offensive player is penalized, his or her team loses yards.

*In extreme cases, players or coaches can be **disqualified**, or thrown out of the game.*

Calculating the damage

The following is a listing of the most common types of fouls and the penalties awarded for each:

Five-yard penalties

offside or encroachment—You may not cross the line of scrimmage before the center snaps the ball.

illegal formation—The players on each team must line up in certain formations. For example, if the offensive team has fewer than seven people on the line of scrimmage, it will receive a penalty.

delay of game—The referee blows a whistle before each down. Once the whistle is blown, the offense may not take more than 25 seconds to snap the ball.

intentional grounding—The quarterback must throw the ball to an intended and eligible receiver. If the quarterback throws the ball away only to avoid being sacked, this foul is called intentional grounding.

Ten-yard penalties

holding—You may not hold or grab any part of your opponent's uniform unless that player has the ball.

hitting a blocker's head—You may not hit a blocker's head.

Fifteen-yard penalties

pulling the face mask—You may not hold onto any part of an opponent's helmet.

late hit—You may not hit or tackle an opponent after the whistle has been blown.

pass interference—A defender cannot hold or stop a receiver in any way until the receiver catches the ball.

fighting—You may not fight with an opponent. In addition to receiving a team penalty, you will be disqualified.

Accept or decline?

The team that benefits from a penalty can **decline**, or reject, it. For example, if the offense throws an incomplete pass and the defense gets a ten-yard penalty, the offense will accept the penalty and move ten yards. However, if the offense completed the pass and gained 23 yards, the offense will decline the penalty because the 23-yard gain from the pass is better than ten yards from the penalty.

Many leagues

The **National Football League**, or **NFL**, is the main American football league. Colleges and high schools also have leagues. Boys and girls can play in local recreational leagues or organized ones such as **Pop Warner**™ leagues. Canadian leagues play a version of football that uses three downs instead of four. Canadian teams have twelve players, and they play on a bigger field.

Football Words

backfield The offensive players who usually handle the ball

conversion A scoring play after a touchdown

down (n) A single offensive play that ends when a ball carrier is tackled or forced out-of-bounds; (adj) Describing a ball carrier whose knee is on the ground

drive A series of plays between the time a team receives the ball and when it loses the ball

eligible receiver An offensive player who is allowed to receive passes

Kansas City Tie-Breaker A system used in youth leagues to break ties, in which each team is given four chances to score from the 10 yard line

line (1) The offensive players that protect the ball carrier by blocking; (2) The defensive players that stop ball carriers from crossing the line of scrimmage

line of scrimmage An imaginary line that marks how far the offense has advanced

pocket An area around the quarterback that linemen try to keep free of opponents

safety (1) A scoring play that occurs when an offensive player with the ball is tackled in his or her own end zone; (2) A defensive player that is the last one between the end zone and the offense

secondary The defensive players that protect against passes and long runs

snap The act of the center giving the ball to a teammate to start a down

special teams The units on a team that play during kickoffs, punts, and field goal attempts

three-point stance Describing a position line players stand in while waiting for the snap

Index